SOUL
WINNING
IN BLACK
CHURCHES

SOUL WINNING IN BLACK CHURCHES

J. HERBERT HINKLE

Baker Book House
Grand Rapids, Michigan

To
Vivian Cooper,
Patricia Rochelle,
and Kathy West

ISBN: 0-8010-4072-8

Printed in the United States of America

PREFACE

I had my first taste of soul winning as a nineteen-year-old pastor. I knocked on doors while pastoring the Greater New Hebrew Baptist Church of Little Rock, Arkansas, and had unusual success: out of thirty families I talked to, ten of them came to our church.

When I went to Chicago Heights, where I pastored the St. Bethel Baptist Church for five years, I became a little complacent about soul winning. I went out only occasionally, and followed no regular schedule (one reason perhaps being that my church was filled). However, I realized I still had a burden to win souls. Although I was preparing to leave my ministry there, I organized a visitation program before moving on.

When I was called to pastor Second Baptist Church of Inkster, Michigan, I promised God that I would fulfill to the best of my ability the

New Testament responsibility. This book is the story of this ministry.

Christian churches and born-again Christians ought to win many souls for Jesus Christ. Churches ought to multiply themselves and grow rapidly, getting lost sinners to repent and trust Christ for salvation. Sadly, I must say that most black churches win few souls, and many, many win none at all. When we compare our church with the New Testament church, it is sad, powerless, fruitless, and cold.

When I speak of the black church, I am not talking about Baptist, Methodist, or Holiness, but all local churches. The message here given crosses all denominational lines or barriers. The truth of the matter is that there is no denomination in the Bible.

When I speak of soul winning I mean bringing a lost sinner to Christ and not simply to church membership. I speak of Christ membership and not church membership; Christianity and not churchianity. Nevertheless, it is my opinion—based on the Word of God—that every saved person ought to be a member of a local church.

Finally, it is my aim in this book to demonstrate the basic cause of failure of soul winning in the black churches. May these observations promote an urgency for soul winning in God's people, as we expectantly await His coming.

CONTENTS

1
A LOOK AT THE BLACK CHURCH

The black church traditionally has been the only real institution in the black neighborhood. The black church grew primarily out of the black man's experience on American soil. Because of its heritage, it was almost impossible for the black church to do anything more than present a "veneer of Christianity." The early church for most blacks was nothing more than a place where one had an opportunity to express the emotions that arose from one's everyday experiences in the American environment. Thus, the religious behavior of the black man and the character of his church have been shaped throughout their development by white patterns as well as by the social and cultural forces within the (so-called) social world of the black man.

ACCEPTANCE INTO THE CHRISTIAN FAITH

The initial opposition to Christianizing the black man tended to disappear when laws made it clear that slaves did not become free through the acceptance of the Christian faith and baptism.

The Anglican church was more reluctant to open her doors to blacks. Although slaves were regularly baptized and taken into the Anglican church during the seventeenth century, it was not until the turning of the eighteenth century that a systematic attempt was made on the part of the established church in England to Christianize the blacks in America. The Society for the Propagation of the Gospel in Foreign Parts was chartered in England in 1701. Through this effort many blacks were saved and accepted into the church.

The missionaries of this society required the prospective members to undergo a period of instruction before being baptized and admitted to communion. Under such circumstances a relatively small and select group of blacks was accepted as converts. Consequently, early in the history of blacks, the church was an institution for the sophisticated and the educated.

Thus, the black man found an opportunity for religious expression in the Baptist and Methodist churches very early in America. Methodists and Baptists expressed an interest in blacks, baptized and proselyted them. These spirited services aroused a favorable response from the blacks. These denominations were successful because of the kinds of services they had. They were especially successful during the revolutionary war.

Emotionalism played a part in the growth of blacks in Methodist and Baptist churches, for blacks found in the fiery messages of salvation a hope and an escape from earthly woes. Moreover, the emphasis which the preachers placed on feeling as a sign of conversion found a ready response in the black slaves who were repressed in so many ways. But there are even more fundamental psychological factors in human nature which offer an explanation of the response of the slaves to the religion of the Methodist and Baptist. The slaves, who had been torn from their homeland and from family and friends, and whose cultural heritage had disintegrated or had lost its meaning in the environment, were broken men. The bonds of a common tradition of religious beliefs and practices had been broken, and the blacks had become "atomized" in the American environment. Here was an appeal, emotional and simple, that provided a new way of life and drew them into a union with their fellow men. It drew them into a common union at first with whites, but later formed a stronger common bond with members of their own black people.

PARTICIPATION OF SLAVES IN RELIGION

During the period of slavery, the blacks in the South participated in the religious life of their masters. This was especially true where the plantations acquired the character of a social as well as industrial institution. Moreover, the house servants often attended the family prayers.

Not all of the religious life of the enslaved blacks was shared with their master. In many places, black preachers were allowed to conduct services among the slaves. Thus, there grew up what has been aptly called "The Invisible Institution," which was encouraged in the areas where the blacks were most isolated from whites. This was the case on larger plantations and in states like Mississippi where the religious education of the slaves was neglected and there were few white ministers who gave their time to blacks. Even in those areas where the various denominations admitted blacks into the churches, the practice of licensing black ministers tended to encourage the growth of the "Invisible Institution." To be sure, the white ministers were never as close to blacks as were the black preachers who sprang up.

Some black people were then allowed to conduct their services in their "own way." With this new privilege came more freedom in expression, and their church services came to be characterized by shouting and other ecstatic forms of religious behavior. Slaves' feelings and attitudes were expressed by such noted preachers as John Jasper, Richard Allen, Absalom Jones, and Nat Turner.

As previously indicated, there were virtually no churches that black people could become a part of, except perhaps for the Baptist and Methodist. Even these churches bounced black people when the number of blacks progressively increased or when white people had no seats.

12

For example, such an event took place, I am told, in 1786, at the St. George Methodist Church in Philadelphia.

From the black church's inception, it has been concerned with freedom of the black man in and out of his church. It has set up outstanding schools to help educate the black boy or girl. I can think of such schools as Philander Smith College, Little Rock, Arkansas; Morehouse College, Spellman College, Arkansas Baptist College, Bishop College, Wiley College, Lemoyne College, and many, many others that have been established to educate black people liberally and religiously. The black church, backing outstanding leaders such as Dr. Martin Luther King, Ralph David Abernathy, and many others, has taken a front seat financially and physically in the whole area of social justice.

As James Cone puts it in his book *Black Theology and Black Power* (incidentally, Cone taught me at Philander Smith College):

> The Black church was the creation of a Black people whose daily existence was an encounter with the overwhelming and brutalizing reality of white power. For the slaves, it was the sole source of personal identity and the sense of the community. Though slaves had no social, economic, or political ties as a people, they had one humiliating factor in common—serfdom! The whole of their being was engulfed in a system intent on their annihilation as persons. Their responses to this overwhelming fact of their existence ranged from suicide to out-

right rebellion. Most refused to accept white Master's definition of Black humanity and rebelled with every ounce of humanity in them. The Black church became the home base for revolution. Some slaves even rebelled to the point of taking up arms against the white world. Others used the church as a means of transporting the slaves to less hostile territory. Northern independent Black churches were "stations in the underground railroads," at which an escaping slave could get means either to become established in the North or to go to Canada—most Blacks used the church as a platform for announcing freedom and equality.

In concluding this chapter, we find that the problems of social injustice and preoccupation with freedom plights have directed the black preacher and the black church toward "social winning" rather than "soul winning."

2

A LOOK AT THE NEW TESTAMENT PATTERN FOR SOUL-WINNING CHURCHES

Most black preachers and black churches think that they really practice what the Bible says if they have a pretty good church and a capable choir. A great number of us do not know much better. A church of this sort is a "pretty good" church when you compare it with other churches of like thinking; but when you compare it to the New Testament church, the church established by Christ, they are very poor representations of a church.

If a preacher has a presentable building (conventional or store front), robed choirs, a good organ and organist, a late model Cadillac, a few nice rags, a diamond ring, a nice pad to live in, and raises plenty of money, he is considered to be somebody. He has a *fine church* compared with another church in the same block. If, however, you compare these well-doing black churches to the New Testament churches as revealed in the Book of Acts, churches in which multiplied thousands were won to Christ in short years, the average black church and pastor will find themselves needing to bow down to ask God to forgive them of their sins and for having failed their community. They will have been responsible for the blood of thousands of lost souls who ought to have been won!

THE PATTERN JESUS SET

What pattern did the Lord Jesus set for us in this matter of soul winning? Jesus called two brothers to leave their nets and follow Him. John sent two of his disciples to question Jesus, and Jesus sent out the seventy two-by-two, teaching that in the mouth of two or three witnesses a truth could be established.

The following verses point up the importance which the Holy Spirit, the author of Scripture, attaches to the ability of *two* to uphold each other: "And he called unto him the twelve, and began to send them forth by two and two" (Mark 6:7). "He sendeth forth two of his disciples" (Mark 11:1). "After these things the Lord appointed other seventy also, and sent them two and two before his face into every city and place, whither he himself would come" (Luke 10:1). In Ecclesiastes 4:9 we read that "two are better than one; because they have good reward for their labour."

OPEN FOR GOD'S BUSINESS SEVEN DAYS A WEEK

I also believe beyond a shadow of doubt that God's divinely appointed way to win the lost is

16

for the church to go out *daily* to witness for Christ.

The Christian religion is a daily business, a full-time job with no vacations or excused time. When I look at most black churches I am distressed to learn that most members feel that Christianity is a matter of Sunday church attendance rather than a daily living for Jesus. Jesus said, "If any man will come after me, let him deny himself, and take up his cross *daily* and follow me" (Luke 9:23). When one really studies the Bible, he is convinced that soul winning was the main business of the early church and not a matter of secondary importance.

It is definitely true that the early church had problems. On occasion it was necessary for their leaders to defy kings (e.g., Peter and John), but they continued to preach Jesus Christ daily. The Bible says, "And daily in the temple, and in every house, they ceased not to teach and preach Jesus Christ" (Acts 5:42). They had a daily fellowship; for they, "continuing daily with one accord in the temple, and breaking bread from *house to house*, did eat their meat with gladness and singleness of heart, praising God, and having favour with all the people. And the Lord added to the church daily such as should be saved" (Acts 2:46, 47).

The early church also carried on the daily ministration of material provision for the saints of God, which necessitated the appointment and election of seven Spirit filled deacons.

The early church launched an all-out campaign to evangelize the known world in their generation; and as a result, the churches were established in the faith and increased in number daily (Acts 16:5). The church today, whether black or white, which is doing God's work in God's way, with God's power and by Scriptural methods, should likewise produce many souls for Christ.

The early church "searched the scriptures daily, whether those things were so" (Acts 17:11), and daily went to publish abroad what they found. Paul "disputed . . . in the market daily with them that met with him" (Acts 17:17) in the city of Athens, and "disputed daily in the school of one Tyrannus" (Acts 19:9) in idolatrous Ephesus.

Now the New Testament church did nothing more than follow Jesus' pattern for soul winning. Jesus said, "Go ye into all the world, and preach the gospel to every creature. He that believeth and is baptized shall be saved; but he that believeth not shall be damned" (Mark 16:15, 16). This means that the members of every local church should take the gospel to every individual in the community. Every church ought to know every saved person and every unsaved person in its community. I am not in the least bit concerned with any limited territory; for, as Dwight L. Moody so aptly stated, "The world is my parish."

Then after they are baptized we are commanded, "Teaching *them* to observe all things whatsoever I have commanded *you.*" That is, the new converts, committed and baptized, are taught to do the same things that we have all been commanded to do—to make disciples. Are there different commands given us than those which were given to the apostles? No! When Peter got somebody saved, he was to urge him to get somebody else saved. Surely, no honest Christian can deny that the main business left the New Testament church by the Savior in the great commission is to win lost souls.

Someone says, "Well, I thought that was just for the preacher." I first want tell you to examine the fact that Jesus sent all disciples two by two, up to seventy in number. Second, I want to raise a basic question, "Isn't it sheep that beget sheep?" Then read Acts 1:15-22:

> And in those days Peter stood up in the midst of the disciples and said, (the number of names together were about an hundred and twenty,) Men and brethren, this scripture must needs have been fulfilled, which the Holy Ghost by the mouth of David spake before concerning Judas, which was guide to them that took Jesus. For he was numbered with us, and had obtained part of this ministry. Now this man purchased a field with the reward of iniquity; and falling headlong, he burst asunder in the midst, and all his bowels gushed out. And it was known unto all the dwellers at Jerusalem; insomuch as that field is called in their proper tongue, Aceldama, that is to say, The field of blood.

For it is written in the book of Psalms, Let his habitation be desolate, and let no man dwell therein; and his bishopric let another take. Wherefore of these men which have companied with us all the time that the Lord Jesus went in and out among us, Beginning from the baptism of John, unto that same day that he was taken from us, *must one be ordained to be a witness with us of his resurrection.*

In Luke 14:23, we are told to go out into highways and hedges, "and compel them to come in, that my house may be filled." Does not this seem that Jesus holds the local church accountable for everyone within possible reach of the gospel?

In Matthew 22:1-14, the servants were instructed to bring in both good and bad to the feast.

NEW TESTAMENT SAINTS SHOULD BE OUR EXAMPLE

The young church in Jerusalem took Jesus' commands literally and followed that program. Wouldn't it be wonderful if preachers today would follow what Jesus said rather than what men have said?

Paul the apostle was a soul winner. He said, "I kept back nothing that was profitable unto you, but have showed you, and have taught you publicly, and from house to house testifying both to the Jews, and also to the Greeks, repentance

20

toward God, and faith toward our Lord Jesus Christ" (Acts 20:20, 21). Again, giving them the example of what they and other Christians should do, he said, "Therefore watch, and remember, that by the space of three years I ceased not to warn everyone night and day with tears" (v. 31). The Bible pattern of witnessing for soul winning is very clearly the pattern for all churches today.

DESPITE PERSECUTION, THE NEW TESTAMENT CHURCHES WON SOULS

Despite problems, they won souls everywhere. Those who were persecuted in Jerusalem were scattered abroad "as far as Phenice, Cyprus, and Antioch" (Acts 11:19). Verse 21 says, "And the hand of the Lord was with them: and a great number believed, and turned unto the Lord." Barnabas came to Antioch a Spirit filled man, "and much people were added to the church" (v. 24)

On a missionary journey, Paul and Barnabas came to Iconium into the synagogue of the Jews and so spoke that a great number both of the Jews and also of the Greeks believed (Acts 14:1). Yes, Christians in the New Testament churches won multitudes of souls, and that on mission fields where we would think conditions most severe. Paul won people in Thessalonica (Acts 17:4), at Berea (Acts 17:12), and at Corinth (Acts 18:8). In a few months a great church was built.

A METHOD FOR THE EARLY CHURCH AND FOR TODAY

The early Christians went from house to house. They did not wait for the world to come to the church, but they went to the world. They went to lost men and women, boys and girls. They won converts from house to house, bringing them to be baptized and to have fellowship with the local church. We should do the same.

Any church that uses the Bible will grow. Let us say you have one hundred members at the present time. If all one hundred would win a soul a month for twelve months and all those souls won would win one, let's see what the number of saved people would be in a year. At the end of the year there would be more than three hundred thousand people won to Christ!

3

MOST BLACK CHURCHES GENERALLY FAIL TO WIN SOULS

If you compare our modern-day churches with the church of the New Testament we can only admit that we have failed to win souls for Christ.

IT IS IMPOSSIBLE FOR LIBERALS, DENIERS OF THE HISTORIC CHRISTIAN FAITH, TO WIN SOULS

One night I was talking to several respected black preachers who said that they felt that the stories of Noah and the ark, Jonah in the whale, and the virgin birth of Jesus were nothing but myths. One of them said to me, "It's all right for you to teach your people that, but don't believe in it." On carrying the conversation further I found that several did not believe in the new birth, the deity of Christ, personally trusting Christ as Savior, nor that Scripture is the authentic, authoritative, and infallible Word of God. There were many other things they didn't believe. In fact, there were so many things they didn't believe that there was scarcely anything left with truth in it that they did believe. These preachers ought to be whipped out of the pulpit! Those false prophets are sinners and could not possibly save anybody.

MOST FORMAL CHURCHES EMPHASIZE CONFIRMATION RATHER THAN CONVERSION

In most of the big-time, sophisticated black churches, neither the preacher nor the people ever think of winning a lost soul. Confirmation takes the place of a conversion experience. Prayers are read from a book. They sound educated and that's about it. Most of these churches want only a certain kind of a person in it—a doctor, a lawyer, or a school teacher. They brag about how quiet the services are and how many big members are in their churches. They maintain good social clubs. There are several of this kind of refrigerated church in our area.

THERE IS NO MENTION OF SOUL WINNING IN BLACK CONVENTIONS

I have been attending the national conventions since 1952 and not one time have I heard anybody mention soul winning. Each year the theme is the same: "The Challenge of This or That"—and most times it boils down to the challenge of getting the president reelected. Once there was a little evangelistic service going on during convention time; but it was nothing but another service with singing, and collection, and preaching. The invitation for discipleship is never extended at the convention. When the preacher gets through entertaining the crowd, everybody jumps up without an invitation, a prayer of benediction, or any report given on the number of souls that have been saved through conventional churches. I never remember hearing a plan of salvation given. I never remember hearing the senior pastors or president calling young men in and training them to become soul winners. I don't know of a single soul-winning pastor or church in the convention.

It is shocking and tragically true that National Baptist churches do not win souls in any way comparable to the record of New Testament churches. It is unbelievable that 6,300,000 people cannot double in a single year. It is unbelievable that 30,000 people will assemble in a city and not one of them can report that they have won a soul during the convention time.

THERE ARE EXCEPTIONS

Thank God, some churches are starting soul-winning programs. I was told that the Jones Evangelistic Association of Philadelphia does engage to some extent in a soul-winning program. This interdenominational body is listed as thirty-second on the list of America's largest Sunday schools.

According to all records, Second Baptist Church of the Bible is the most active and productive black soul-winning church in the world.

July 1969 we had 536 people registered; in January 1972 our registration was over 1,500. We had 62 people in Sunday school in December 1969; we had 1,100 enrolled with a record attendance of 1,226 and an average of 560 students from January to May 1972. We expect to have as many as 700 to 800 students every Sunday commencing with November, and we are expecting 1,500 per Sunday average by 1973 in Sunday school. May I also insert the fact that we minister to more people for the preaching than we do for Sunday school.

Because of preaching and teaching and advertising, there are several other churches that are now catching on to the soul-winning programs.

We receive our inspiration from the Holy Bible, particularly the Book of Acts. We receive inspiration and encouragement from Temple Baptist Church, First Baptist Church at Hammond, the Cathedral of Tomorrow, the Akron Baptist Temple, and many other churches. We dream of being one of the ten largest Sunday schools someday. Of course, we know that we have our work cut out for us when we note that according to Elmer Towns's article in the August 1970 issue of *Christian Life*, First Baptist Church, Hammond, Indiana, reported 5,002 conversions in 1969, followed by 3,165 at Gilead Baptist Church, Allen Park, Michigan; 2,300 at Highland Park Baptist Church, Chattanooga, Tennessee; 2,267 at Landmark Baptist Temple, Cincinnati, Ohio; and 1,893 at Thomas Road Baptist Church, Lynchburg, Virginia.

4
INTERNAL CRISES
IN BLACK CHURCHES

The average member of a black church would like to see a few more people saved—providing he doesn't have to go out and get them. The members feel that if they get a really top-notch preacher, he can turn the community upside down and all the people will come running down to their church. They do not want to be looked down on as being holy or fanatical, they do not want others to think they are different, they do not like to change much. They want the church to be a nice social club—never embarrassing anybody about death or hell; and they don't like any demands on the old-timers of the community.

But the simple fact is that most black churches do not win souls because they are not set up to win souls! Soul winning is ignored in the plans and organization of our churches. You will never hear a member in a black church making out any group plans to go soul winning.

But we love to organize for spiritual and social entertainment.

To be perfectly earnest with you from experience, there is no halfhearted, easy way to win a multitude of souls. There is no way to have a great soul-winning church without prayer, without faith, without sacrifice, and without a drastic revolution in the organizational aims, programs, plans, and administration of the church.

Our program, our plans, our emphasis is not that of the great New Testament soul-winning churches that the Bible clearly describes for us to follow.

Most churches want a man who is fairly well educated, a pretty good preacher, and one who pulls close to an "A" in personal appearance. His ministerial duties as far as the average member is concerned is to preach the Word, to give them an enjoyable church program, to marry their children, to comfort them when they are sick, and to bury their dead. I have never gone to a church where any officer asked about my position as a pastor in getting lost souls saved. Most preachers and churches have forgotten the Scripture that asks, "What man of you, having an hundred sheep, if he lose one of them, doth not leave the ninety and nine in the wilderness, and go after that which is lost, until he find it?" (Luke 15:4).

Some churches think the pastor's work is to preach on Sunday morning and Sunday night, conduct a mid-week prayer meeting, and pick up the ladies who want a ride to the missionary society or washeteria. Some people think the preacher ought to be in all the community affairs from PTA meetings to the Elks Lodge.

It is true what Deacon Wallace of Chicago Heights used to quote frequently: "Feed my lambs" (John 21:15) and twice "Feed my sheep" (John 21:16, 17). And Peter did just that, too. When he preached a soul-winning message at Pentecost and along with the testimony of many others, he saw some three thousand people claim the power of the Holy Ghost and all were baptized.

But don't forget, my brothers and sisters, the parable of the lost sheep. The one lost sheep was as much his sheep as were the safe ninety and nine. And remember that Jesus told the woman of Canaan that He was sent "unto the lost sheep of the house of Israel" (Matt. 15:24). Often the Lord Jesus looked on the poor lost multitude and had compassion on them, for "they were as sheep not having a shepherd" (Mark 6:34). The principal duty of every shepherd is to seek first the lost one, even if he has to leave the ninety and nine in the wilderness.

In Ephesians the Lord tells about the work of the preachers, whether they are apostles, prophets, evangelists, or teachers. After reading the following verses, the goals of the church should be well established in your mind.

> And he gave some, apostles; and some, prophets; and some, evangelists; and some, *pastors and teachers*; For the perfecting of the saints, for the work of the ministry, for

the edifying of the body of Christ: Till we all come in the unity of the faith, and of the knowledge of the Son of God, unto a perfect man, unto the measure of the stature of the fulness of Christ: That we henceforth be no more children, tossed to and fro, and carried about with every wind of doctrine, by the sleight of men, and cunning craftiness, whereby they lie in wait to deceive; But speaking the truth in love, may grow up into him in all things, which is the head, even Christ: From whom the whole body fitly joined together and compacted by that which every joint supplieth, according to the effectual working in the measure of every part, maketh increase of the body unto the edifying of itself in love. —Eph. 4:11-16

In most black churches the deacons try to run things. These men are called deacons, but they are actually demons who know about as much concerning their job as described in the Bible as I know about flying a super jet in combat. They have never been taught; they have never tried to learn; they don't want to know. They have no intention of learning, and therefore they could never win a soul to anything but the devil. As a matter of fact, I would venture to say that most of the deacons I have met have never been converted according to Scripture, even though all of them claim to "have religion."

Would you believe that in the average black church the deacon does not attend Sunday school, Bible class, or any other kind of class where he can learn God's Word? Would you believe that the average deacon does not carry

30

his Bible to any services? Would you believe that the average deacon does not know anything about the Bible? Would you believe that the average deacon has never heard of soul winning? Would you believe the average deacon does not tithe?

As far as he knows, his duties are (1) to watch the pastor, (2) to keep peace and to stand between the pastor and church, (3) to count the money, (4) to attend arguing meetings, (5) to keep the church from putting too many irons in the fire, (6) to look out for the "po" member or the sick member who needs a little assistance, and (7) to help call a pastor when the pastor leaves. He has never read Acts 6. He thinks, therefore, that since the people elected him, he is the watchdog. Generally, he tries to stay in with a few cliques in the church so that when he wants to kill some future issue, he has a spokesman or a person to challenge it. When he is against something, he runs to the pastor first and tells him that the people have "been talking." Most times he is the leader and talker of the people.

I thank God for the Christian men He has given me to work with here at Second Baptist Church of the Bible. Here, men know their job and are willing to learn the Word of God. They follow leadership, and this has been to a great extent the secret of our success thus far.

When Moses' arms were heavy in days of old, God gave to him Aaron and Hur to hold his hands high. Aaron got on one side; Hur, on the other. Each lifted one of Moses' arms high. When his arms were lifted, the battle was won. When his arms were lowered, the battle was lost (Exod. 17:12). God has, in His wisdom, given to pastors today in the New Testament church men of God called deacons, who lift the hands of the pastor, work with him, and serve God with him in loyal, sacrificial service to the church and to the Savior.

It is said of Saul, the first king of Israel, shortly after he was anointed, "And Saul also went home to Gibeah; and there went with him a group of men, whose hearts God had touched" (I Sam. 10:26). How much easier it is for a pastor to serve the Lord Jesus Christ when it can be said of him that there went with him a band of men—deacons, if you please—whose hearts God had touched. Even the Savior, our Lord Jesus Christ, chose twelve men to work with Him, stand beside Him, walk with Him, and learn from Him in His work of redemption.

Here are the qualifications of deacons at Second Baptist Church of the Bible:

1. I Timothy 3:8-13: "Likewise must the deacons be grave, not double-tongued, not given to much wine, not greedy of filthy lucre; Holding the mystery of the faith in a pure conscience. *And let these also first be proved;* then let them use the office of a deacon, being found blameless. Even so must their wives be grave, not slanderers, sober, faithful in all things. Let the deacons be the husband of one wife, ruling their

children and their own houses well. For they that have used the office of a deacon well purchase to themselves a good degree, and great boldness in the faith which is in Christ Jesus." His wife ought to meet the qualifications in these last three verses.

2. A man must be a member of Second Baptist Church of the Bible at least one year prior to being considered for a deacon. He must attend prayer meeting and Bible study regularly.

3. A man must attend Sunday school regularly, as well as morning and evening services.

4. A man must be a tither.

5. A man must be a soul winner (active participation).

Let me pause to add that we do not accept a man from another church as a deacon just because he was a deacon in the other church. We accept each man on an equal basis according to his qualifications, his devotion, and his service to the Lord Jesus Christ.

We do not accept a man to be a deacon because of his financial standing. That is not taken into consideration. We do not take into consideration a man's social standing in the community. He might be a school teacher, a doctor, an attorney, or just a big wheel. That does not give him one bit of preference over the poorest man. We use only Biblical and spiritual qualifications.

6. A man must live a separated life. If we know that he is the city's number one party

leader, or gambler, or drinker, we will not consider him for a deacon of Second Baptist Church of the Bible.

The deacons of our church are my helpers. The main relationship of a deacon is to be a pal and to offer encouragement to the pastor. They actually help work with sick and shut-ins; they help in developing plans for the future; they prayerfully consider the direction of our church; they consider the buying of property, the drawing up of the budget, the construction of buildings, and so forth. As a result they recommend the best program that is suited to the church.

At Second Baptist Church of the Bible, there are no dual boards. We simply have one board: the board of deacons. Since we are a corporation under the laws of our state, we must have trustees. These trustees are chosen from the deacon board. By virtue of the fact that our chairman of the deacon board is also the president of the corporation, he is a trustee. These trustees have no authority. They have no meetings. They simply fill an honorary position, fulfilling the laws required by the state of Michigan. Why have two boards when the board of deacons can care for the needs of the church?

Let me allow you to read what Brother Henderson Hendricks, the chairman of our deacons here at Second Baptist Church of the Bible, has to say about the one board idea, our facilities, our finance plan, and our pastor.

> The idea of having one board is the best policy in the church if peace is to prevail.

When there are two boards, deacons and trustees, more trouble exists because each board thinks it is more important than the other. Each believe that they should have the authority to do as they see fit. When told the limitations of their authority, confusion may develop within the church.

Oftentimes when business meetings are called, one board will try to sway the members of the church to their way of thinking. There is always "one weakminded" member of the board posted to start an argument, backed up by the members of the board on whose behalf he is speaking, even though he may be wrong. This causes a split and much confusion between the two boards, which in turn splits the church.

The Bible does not support trustees. They *are not* mentioned in the Bible. Trustees have been added by man. The deacon board is the *only one* supported by the Bible.

It has been a pleasure working with one board. There is more unity, love, and better understanding between men.

ADVICE TO OTHER CHAIRMEN

My advice to other chairmen is to be ever gentle, kind, and understanding. Learn each man's attitude and work with him on his level. Let there be no secrets among the board members concerning church thoughts. I believe that there will always be peace, harmony, and love among brethren with this theory. I have found that these practices foster successful leadership.

Facilities

In a church where you expect to grow, you must have good facilities. It is not logical to ask people to come to any building without the facilities to accommodate them. Our facilities at the present time are not up to par, but we are building a new edifice with facilities to accommodate our needs as a growing and soul-winning church. The purpose of the church is to win souls to Christ. For He said, "If I be lifted up, I will draw all men unto me." He said again, "Go out into the highways and hedges, and compel them to come." He said also, "Let your light so shine that men might see your good works." Therefore we must prepare our facilities in order that they, along with our ministries, will perpetuate our soul-winning program.

Our Finance Plan

Our plan for financing whatever we do in the church is directed through tithes and offerings. This is the only plan that the Bible teaches for the support of the church. This is what our pastor, Rev. Hinkle, teaches; and this is what we believe and do. Since we have cut out all the gimmicks and begging, and replaced them with only tithes and offerings, our finances have increased by more than 500 percent. We are certain that we will progress as we continue to accept God's way.

Bus Ministry and Cost

It is true that it costs much to operate a bus ministry, but the souls you win are worth the cost of operating the buses. We now have ten buses. And we have brought as many as 297 people to church on Sunday who would not have come had it not been for the bus ministry. We don't mind the cost of the bus ministry as long as we get the people to come to Christ. If we are able to bring the people to hear the Word of God, it is worth the cost.

OUR PROGRAM

Our program here at Second Baptist Church of the Bible has been wonderful since our pastor presented it to us in December of 1969. It has been an inspiration to the entire church. It has provided unity, cooperation, more love, peace, and understanding for our church. The people work better together because of this program.

OUR PASTOR

I could not conclude without mentioning the real reason for our success, which is our pastor, Rev. J. Herbert Hinkle, who has been a real asset to the church. He has taught love, unity, understanding, and endurance. He has preached forbearance, humility, and forgiveness for everyone. Not only has he taught this, it has been seen in him. He has lived what he has preached. Let us all pray that God will continue to bless him in his ministry and leadership.

Deacon H. Hendricks
Chairman of Deacons
Second Baptist Church of the Bible

In most black churches, visiting the sick is about the only kind of visitation program that exists. Some call it missionary work. Some pastors would be heavy-hearted and their congregations impoverished if the blessings of God on the church depended on how much they gave to sick folk or to missionary work. The pastor visits the sick and organizes a mission meeting in the community, but does no soul winning! I know many hundreds of churches that have ignored the order which the Lord Himself gave: "But ye shall receive power, after that the Holy Ghost is come upon you: and ye shall be witnesses unto me both in Jerusalem, in all Judea, and in Samaria, and unto the uttermost part of the earth" (Acts 1:8). The Bible emphasizes visiting for souls "daily in the temple, and in every house they ceased not to teach and preach Jesus Christ" (Acts 5:42).

Most black pastors *in the North* will visit sick members. Most *black pastors in the South don't even go to church except for a program or some kind of special meeting.* Many churches do no visiting other than that of visiting a sick member.

Brother pastor, let me point out what the Bible says about sick visitation: "Is any sick among you? let him call for the elders of the church; and let them pray over him, anointing him with oil in the name of the Lord: And the prayer of faith shall save the sick, and the Lord shall raise him up; and if he have committed sins, they shall be forgiven him" (James 5:14, 15).

When I went to college, there was no emphasis on soul winning. Colleges are more interested in teaching Hebrew, Greek, philosophy, and homiletics. Unfortunately, I don't know any schools that teach preachers how to win souls. They are taught formal worship services, expository preaching, but are not taught how to have a revival, how to give an invitation, how to build a strong soul-winning visitation program, how to win hundreds through the Sunday school.

Note that most sermons that are preached follow the basic Pastor's Manual each year. They have suggestions for Christmas, Palm Sunday, Ash Wednesday, Good Friday, Easter, Mother's Day, Father's Day, Memorial Day, and Thanksgiving. More often than not, they incorporate meaningless speeches and children's jokes, rather than sending inspired thoughts. These books teach preachers to be occupied with routine administrative matters and keeping church people happy, with very little emphasis on soul winning.

National Baptist Convention U.S.A., Inc., National Progressive Convention, Inc., National Baptist Convention of America, Inc., all say much about the denominational program, about schools, about the challenge of the age, about the mission work in Africa, about retirement, civil rights, and the annual meetings; but they say nothing to black pastors about soul winning. The professors at most of our institutions of religious learning are not soul winners. They are great critics of evangelists' preachings. Most of the professors mock at any special fervor about preaching, or tears, or holy enthusiasm. They would criticize the emotion in my preaching.

Many of them are simply ruining young men with theories.

There are some black churches that are like refrigerators: freezing cold. Your presence is but a mere visit if you are not one of the elite. For no one shakes your hand nor invites you to do anything in the church. These churches are formal. Their services are given by the denominational committee or ordered through the mail or copied directly from a book. Their music comes from a concert at the nearest opera house.

Often some big-time black churches have a "junior church." The regular auditorium type service is so stiff, formal, and cold that little children do not understand or appreciate it; so these children are sent to the basement where they are taught how to be part of a cold church.

I was invited to a certain cold, God-forgotten church and was asked three weeks in advance what my choir would be singing. A girl from the congregation was invited to the pulpit to introduce me. The title of the doxology with the key that it was to be played in was listed on the program. Formal, noncordial, stiff-necked ushers were asked to escort me. The church was quiet, with very few Amens given. They called everybody doctor, professor, attorney, and so forth. This church and many others like it would never invite anybody to win a soul for Christ. They would never go looking for poor folk. They forgot the words of Jesus: "The Spirit of the Lord is upon me, because he hath anointed me to preach the gospel to the poor" (Luke 4:18).

Let me give a warning to you preachers of this country. If your church is of a caliber where a man cannot feel at home without a tie and a new suit, you are not going to see many souls won. Brother preacher, let's forget this formal bit and let's get somebody saved. Let's make our services warm and friendly. Let's make God the center of our worship.

5

BLACK CHURCHES GENERALLY HAVE TOO MANY AUXILIARIES

In most black churches the popular thing to do is have many auxiliaries to give everybody something to do. Some preachers take in a member this way: "Thank you, sister, for coming forward. Do you have anything to tell the folk?" She answers, "Yes, sir. I want you all to know, sisters and brothers, that the Lord freed my soul; and I promised Him that I would serve Him till I die." Or, "I know I been born again. I didn't make no mistake about it, and I just want to join the church." The pastor then asks, "Are you sure you got religion?" She hollers, "Yes, sir!" The pastor says, "Ain't that wonderful! You got to know it for yourself. Brother, after hearing the testimony of this applicant, what you say?"

One of the big deacons or one that wants to be seen will hand the answer. "I motion that we accept the testimony of the applicant, and after the right hand of fellowship, she be given all rights and privileges as any other member." (If she is a candidate for baptism, insert "baptism.") The preacher answers, "You have heard the motion. Any question?" Congregation: "Question." Preacher: "All in favor answer by your usual Aye." Congregation: "Aye."

The pastor shakes her hand, giving her the right hand of fellowship and asking what auxiliary she would like to work with or what auxiliary she used to work with. He sends her to that auxiliary. No instructions about salvation, soul winning, Christ, or orientation.

Here are a list of auxiliaries in the average black church: Benevolent Club; Minister's, Deacons,' Trustees,' Mother's Boards; Missionary Society; Nurses' Guild number 1 and number 2; senior, young adult, youth, and children's choirs; gospel chorus; male chorus; Sunday school; B.T.U.; Ushers' Board number 1, number 2, and number 3; Deaconesses; Ever Ready Club; Willing Workers; Ministers' Wives; Worker's Council; Youth Council; Youth Missionary; Young Matrons; Red Circle; Brotherhood; and Beautifying Club.

Each president becomes a pastor; and whatever he doesn't like about the church program, he organizes the whole group against it—right or wrong. When they get angry because of no response, they go home or refuse to serve. If the church wants to visit another church and it doesn't fit in with their plans, all of them refuse to go. If one person acts indifferent, all of them act indifferent. If one talks in church, all of them talk in church. I have preached soul-saving revivals for churches while the auxiliaries have held their meetings elsewhere in the church building, leaving without even coming to the revival. I have seen them stay out of the service half the night, coming in only when the invitation is being extended.

In most black churches the pastor says only, "The doors of the church are open." No plan of salvation is explained and extended. Auxiliaries do nothing but divide a church. People become more in love with their groups than they do with God and His church. These organizations were put in the church primarily to raise money, not to save souls; not for evangelistic reasons, not for missionary purposes, not to teach the people righteousness or the Bible: only to raise money.

Some preachers brag about the fact that they have a meeting going on every night at the church. This means nothing. These auxiliary presidents or the preachers need to let the families have some free time so they can come out to Bible class and learn what they are supposed to do for God. It would be a major project to save most of the people in auxiliaries; for most of them don't know the plan of salvation, nor have they ever really been saved.

In most black churches we have majored on minor things and minored on major things. We have concentrated on the church work instead of the Work of the church. We have our auxiliaries selling chicken, barbecue, ice cream, dressing, fish, candy, and so forth, instead of teaching

44

people about the Bible. A church is to be supported by tithes and offerings. Let's cut out those groups majoring in money raising and institute a soul-winning program. Jesus gave you plenty to do: "Preach and teach" in every house.

One one occasion, one of my associates and I went to one of the largest churches in Chicago. The pastor told us that the secret of the success and growth of his church was that the people were not really pressured to follow the Bible in giving but could give whatever they wanted to give, as long as they joined an auxiliary. They did not teach tithing but giving of dues in the auxiliary. Each club in that church was given a Sunday to have an anniversary to raise money by any means possible, as long as it was morally sound. They have fifty-two auxiliaries or clubs. He said, "You know, you've got to get the money some way. Our system is just as good as tithing." (He actually thinks he has invented a system as good as Jehovah God's.) They raise two hundred dollars that way on a Sunday morning. But they will never be the soul winners they could be. That pastor doesn't fight tithing, but he doesn't practice it either. Jesus said, "I know you are either for me or against me." I say, let's cut out all unworthy projects that are really only junk, as well as unnecessary groups, and institute a soul-winning program.

6

MOST BLACK PREACHERS
THINK PREACHING IS "IT"

One of the upsetting things about black pastors is that they are not really concerned about winning souls. They would like to have more church members, but they are not interested in winning souls for Christ. Many black churches in the South have an opportunity to see their pastor only once a month, and once every other week in many churches. The pastor is happy if he has a pretty fair building, gets plenty to eat when in town, and has no pastoral problem until he sees them again. Most of these pastors don't know what it is to see their church until their "Pastoral Sunday."

Brother black pastor, I don't care how much you talk about soul winning, evangelism, and so forth; I don't care what you say; nobody knows this any better than I: a pastor who does not personally win souls will not make soul winners of others. The man who does not have burden enough and power enough to win souls personally, will not have the burden and power he needs in the pulpit. Every pastor ought to be a great soul winner. One who does not practice soul winning will not preach soul winning effectively.

If black pastors would try, they could do it. Yes, I certainly do mean that. I see so many people who come forward in our church on Sundays that I have personally won to Christ.

What is the secret? There is no secret other than believing the Bible and including in your busy schedule a few hours a week to soul win. You must seek and ask God for the Holy Ghost's power. You could win more than your church wins now. Brethren, let's face a basic truth—the failure in our churches is, first of all, a pastor failure. There is no way to build great soul-winning churches without soul-winning pastors. Here is the first and easiest key to building great soul-winning black churches. You must get on fire for God; you must love precious souls; you must have love to see a man saved; you must go after the man next door. If you become a faithful soul winner, your church will change. If you have problems in your church, try soul winning. If you can't draw anybody, start soul winning. If your church is cold, nonspiritual, or dead, start soul winning.

Reverend, you say you don't have a gift, you can't do it? Wait! Do you really believe that any fervent, Spirit filled pastor who sets aside time to pray and to actually seek lost people could not win souls every month? It is not a lot of gifts and education that are needed in the pulpit, but it takes Jesus and a love for souls.

Do you understand what the "call to preach" means? Some preachers would win more souls if they were not hung up on the fact that God called them to preach—not to knock on doors. Some pastors reason (Biblically, they think) that "called to preach" means to stand in a pulpit and preach to a church full of people. They certainly do not understand the Bible and particularly Mark 16:15-16. Jesus makes it rather clear that we are commanded to "go ye into all the world, and preach the gospel to every creature." Now, I believe I am called to preach to large crowds; but even then I believe I am responsible for making the gospel simple enough to be understood by every creature. So I preach whether I am talking to one man, two men, or hundreds of men. Let's take another look at Mark 16:15-16. Did Jesus say, "Go ye into every congregation and every baptized church"? Do you know what it means to preach to every creature—not to a certain kind of man, but to a man? Preach—win that soul! This commission indicates that public preaching is not just "IT," but that Jesus wants you to preach to the man next door, at the barber shop, service station, cleaners, and so forth. Maybe you ought to read the parable in Luke 14:17-24.

Was Jesus a soul winner? Jesus preached to multitudes; but He also preached to Nicodemus, the woman of Sychar, blind Bartimaeus, Zacchaeus, the woman at Simon's house, the

48

woman taken in adultery. Isn't He our example in that area also?

Some preachers have never tried to win a soul, and therefore they don't know how to do it. But how can a pastor who does not clearly see how to win a soul teach his members how to do it? And how can he have a great soul-winning church? He may have history and theology in his preaching, but there will be little fire and power.

You can win a soul if you can humble yourself and come down where the people are—if you can talk to people. You can win them if you go and get them and compel them to make that step to Jesus Christ. People are glad to see someone who will talk to them—one of whom they can ask questions they wouldn't dare ask in church or in a formal situation.

Gentlemen, preaching alone is not "IT." Some fellows think that preaching is all you need. Some ignorant preachers say that all you need to do is "cry out" like John and God will send them running. Well, such preachers don't know much about Scripture. For the Bible says, "Go ye into all the world"; "Go to the hedges and highways and compel them to come in, so that my house may be filled"; "If you come after me, deny yourself and take up your cross daily and follow me"; "And daily in the temple and in every house they ceased not to teach and preach Jesus Christ . . . praising God and having favor with all the people, the Lord added daily such as should be saved."

There are many other texts that I could point out to you about the "IT" of the church.

Most black preachers are more concerned about how good they sound than how many souls are saved. One of the tragic things that happens to many of my brothers is that they spend most of their time trying to develop an appealing sound rather than a sound appeal. I have known fellows to be considered outstanding preachers because they had a good singing voice—and for no other reason. Now, let me make it clear that I am not against a man having a pleasant voice. I certainly can't stand a broken down voice or a man who neglects to project, but I am against a man who has only a voice and no message. A pleasant voice is worthwhile in most professions, but so is knowledge; and in the ministry, so is the Holy Ghost.

Good sounding preachers usually do not have any stern messages. They usually choose popular titles like: "Why I Sing the Blues," "Someday We'll Be Together," "I Love You, Baby," and so forth. A whole lot of worldly topics will not produce godly people. A church without godly people will not soul win. In most black churches where pastors are busy seeking a crowd rather than bringing a man under condemnation for sin, letting him know that if he dies unsaved he is going to hell, you will find that worldly people are entrenched in the church. They have kin people in the church. They will put anybody in a position of church leadership, without any consideration of God's will in the matter.

50

You cannot take sinners and build a saved church. Make preaching plain but Spirit filled (not only emotionally) in order that your church will win the support of born-again Christians. This kind of preaching will cause a revolution in the church. You may even lose a few members. I try at our church to preach the Word, and I expect some members to be upset. I expect to make enemies because of my stand on the Word, but I will never refuse to preach it as God has given it to me. If I lose here, God will put me somewhere else where I can win. I know that the black church is accustomed to hearing very little of the "real" gospel preached. We preach Dry Bones in the Valley, Eagle Stirreth up Her Nest, The Prodigal Son, Ball Game of Life, Daniel in the Lions' Den, and so forth.

One of the greatest needs in black churches is not more civil rights organizations, United Nations or social-economic groups, but soul-winning messages to workers who are challenged and instructed.

You cannot win souls if you do not know your stand on vital issues. Some issues I speak of are the virgin birth, Jonah and the whale, evolution, the deity of Christ, His bodily resurrection, and so forth.

Education alone won't do it, either. You cannot get people save simply by talking about Plato, Thales, Heraclitus, and so forth. You may have a crowd to preach to: doctors, lawyers, professional people of all stripes. But remember, God also wants the man on the streets, the housewife, the high school student, and the child. It is terrible but true: there are many preachers and churches that want only a certain kind of person in their club (church). So much pride will not permit the Holy Ghost to do His work.

Brother preacher, you have plenty to talk about that the common man wants and needs to know. Preach on hell, on judgment, adultery, drunkenness, divorce, war, death, and similar vital subjects.

Shout a little for God. Don't be so quiet—or what we call dignified.

(1) Cut your listeners to the heart: Acts 2:37; 7:54.
(2) Preach the Word constantly: II Timothy 4:2.
(3) Rebuke sharply, that they may be sound in the faith: Titus 1:10-13.

The command in Isaiah 58:1 is "Cry aloud, spare not, lift up thy voice like a trumpet, and show my people their transgression, and the house of Jacob their sins." In this last third of the twentieth century, God is still the same, man is the same, sin is the same; therefore, God's mercy is the same. You can never expect God to deal with people on a Biblical basis when you don't teach or preach the Bible.

Many preachers go to school and graduate with nothing more than book knowledge of the

Holy Spirit. They know nothing of His working power whatsoever. We need to know God and the Holy Spirit, and our sermons need to reflect the fact that we know God.

Isaiah spoke of Jesus in prophecy, and Jesus fulfilled his promise when He announced that "the Spirit of the Lord is upon me, because he hath anointed me to preach the gospel" (Luke 4:18). Jesus' gospel was powerful because it was Spirit filled. The disciples became powerful preachers when the Holy Ghost came on them (promised in Luke 24:49; Acts 1:8). In Acts 2:4 and 4:31 we hear about the same people at a later time, that "when they prayed, the place was shaken where they were assembled together; and they were all filled with the Holy Ghost."

Paul was converted; then the preacher prayed that he would be filled with the Holy Ghost (Acts 9:17). Barnabas, the great soul winner, was full of the Holy Ghost and of faith: Acts 11:24. John the Baptist was filled from his mother's womb with the Holy Ghost (Luke 1:15-16). That's why he was a great soul winner.

Gentlemen, I am afraid that one of the reasons most of us don't win souls is because we have not had a personal experience with God. Many of us have a zeal for God, but not according to knowledge. Being ignorant of God's righteousness, we have tried to establish our own righteousness. We don't want to be criticized or called fanatics or extremists. We are not filled with the Holy Ghost. Most black preachers seek only to do church work and never think about the Work of the church. I wish you could get on fire for God. If you did, it would change the structure of our black churches. It would change the people; it would make us fruitful Christians rather than fruitless ones.

Let us get busy doing the work God has left here for us to do, rather than just sitting around pleasing people.

7

SINGING IN BLACK CHURCHES IS FILLED WITH SOUL BUT DOES NOT WIN SOULS

Everyone will agree that no other church choir or singing congregation can compare in soul with what one finds in the black church. Our feelings and our emotions cannot be surpassed. The singing found in most Baptist or Holiness black churches is contrary to the formalistic, cold, dull, and anemic singing of other groups.

Despite the fact that our singing is filled with soul and emotion, it very seldom wins a born-again soul to our church. Granted, the singing sounds good. There are many good black groups such as the Soul Stirrers, the Clouds of Joy, the Caravans, the Davis Sisters, and so forth; but I am sure none of these good gospel groups can boast of having a soul-winning program. I doubt whether any of these groups have knocked on doors. I doubt whether members of these groups regularly attend services at any church, other than perhaps the one in which they are singing.

Sad as it sounds, we are more concerned about how "tuff" we look, how "tuff" we sing, rather than about what we sing or who hears us sing. Some groups commit a blasphemous sin to God by the way they perform or by the extreme manner in which they conduct themselves in worship. I have witnessed many guest choirs in action. As soon as they had finished singing, they walked out (even during the preaching time or invitational time). This is ridiculous!

Songs in the black church have traditionally been songs with messages of heartaches and pain, trouble and sadness (rightly so because of slavery). Let's look at a few songs that we sing: "Sometimes I Feel Like a Motherless Child," "When the Storms of Life Are Raging," "I'll Be So Glad When I Get Home," "Lord, I'm a Poor Pilgrim of Sorrow," "I Know the Lord Will Make a Way Somehow," and many others.

Be assured that my feeling toward these songs reflects in no way a lack of understanding of the black community. I was born black, I am black, and I will always remain black; but I do think we can stop singing some of these troubled songs and sing songs with messages of hope and comfort. Songs like "My Faith Looks Up to Thee," "On Christ the Solid Rock I Stand," "Have Thine Own Way, Lord," "Softly and Tenderly," "Jesus, Keep Me Near the Cross," "Draw Me Nearer," "What a Friend We Have in Jesus," and "Is Your Heart Right with Jesus?" are songs of hope and comfort. I am not saying that we should dismiss all of the sad songs that we sing,

56

but we should minimize them. We ought not to give up our heritage, but supplement it with some solid songs of faith and hope.

I am not saying we should replace all of our traditional songs with anthems, because you cannot build a soul-winning church on anthems. Anthems are sufficient for a concert or a formal, superficial service. However, in a church that sings nothing but anthems, the preacher and people are tranquilized before the sermon, instead of being aroused and inspired to soul winning. The music of a church must set an atmosphere for soul winning.

I am spending time here to explain that a Christian church needs a variety of good music. I don't want to be misunderstood or to sound trite, but I believe that there is a time and place for everything. I agree strongly with Dr. Martin Luther King when he said that we have two different kinds of churches in black America: "one that burns with emotionalism and another that freezes with classicism." The former, reducing worship to entertainment, places more emphasis on volume than on content and confuses spirituality with muscularity. The danger in such a church is that the members may have more religion in their hands and feet than in their hearts and souls. At midnight this type of church has neither the vitality nor the relevant gospel to feed hungry souls.

The other type of Negro church that feeds no midnight traveler has developed a class system and boasts of its dignity, its membership of professional people, and its exclusiveness. In such a church the worship service is cold and meaningless, the music dull and uninspiring, and the sermon little more than a homily on current events. If the pastor says very much about Jesus Christ, the members feel that he is robbing the pulpit of dignity. If the choir sings Negro spirituals, the members claim an affront to their class status. This type of church tragically fails to recognize that worship at its best is a social experience in which people from all levels of life come together to affirm their oneness and unity under God.

So you see, we must be on our guard not to have a church that falls in either of these extreme categories. I am against a church that places total emphasis on emotions and jumping and shouting. Some of my people once visited such a church with me, where a young man performing repeatedly sang, "Why don't you? Think about it! Why don't you? Think about it! Why don't you? Think about it!" and so forth. This "gospel rumbo" went on for about ten to fifteen minutes. Finally I turned to someone near me and asked, "Think about what?" The person answered that we are supposed to think about the fact that there is a God somewhere. Only with this answer did that particular gospel rumbo attain a meaning. I am also against a cold, dull church whose members are more concerned about keeping their clothes intact or about how professional they are, rather than about yearning for lost souls. These types of churches emphasize that their pastors have degrees rather than salvation; have personality rather than ability to live by the principles of God's Holy Word. They never want any sermons preached that will offend them. They talk about God's goodness and ignore God's wrath. Yes, a church ought to be decent and orderly, but it also must be spiritual and saved.

Musical instruments were used to praise God Jehovah in the Holy Bible. The Book of Psalms tells us: "Praise ye the Lord. Sing unto the Lord a new song, and his praise in the congregation of saints. Let Israel rejoice in him that made him: let the children of Zion be joyful in their King. Let them praise his name in the dance: let them sing praises unto him with the timbrel and harp" (149:1-3). Psalm 150 tells us: "Praise ye the Lord. Praise God in his sanctuary: praise him in the firmament of his power. Praise him for his mighty acts: praise him according to his excellent greatness. Praise him with the sound of the trumpet: praise him with the psaltery and harp. Praise him with the timbrel and dance: praise him with stringed instruments and organs. . . . Praise him upon the high sounding cymbals. Let every thing that hath breath praise the Lord. Praise ye the Lord." II Samuel 6:5 tells us: "And David and all the house of Israel played before the Lord on all manner of instruments made of fir wood, even on harps, and on psalteries, and on timbrels, and on cornets, and on cymbals." You may also read I Chronicles 15:28; II Chronicles 29:25; I Corinthians 14:7

in order to paint a more vivid picture of the use of musical instruments in the Bible to praise God.

I certainly believe that musical instruments have a place in the service of praise and may be used of the Spirit of God for great spiritual blessings, but our musical instruments are not used to win souls. When Saul, the king of Israel, became sad, he had David, the shepherd boy, come to play for him. "And it came to pass, when the evil spirit from God was upon Saul, that David took an harp, and played with his hand: so Saul was refreshed, and was well, and the evil spirit departed from him" (I Sam. 16:23).

Thus we have evidence that musical instruments can be used by the Spirit of God. However, there are certain limitations imposed by tradition which often hinder the soul-winning use of instruments and music in the house of God. For example, some churches emphasize pipe organ or other instruments that are excellent for formalistic liturgies and services in modernistic churches, but are unsatisfactory for evangelistic services.

In some churches there has been traditionally more emphasis on prelude and postlude than there has been on interlude. Most of these churches are concerned about the key that a number is written in and are very conscious when a soloist makes a mistake. Professionalized music may tend to promote what is called "culture," but it does not tend to promote soul winning. There is a great need for music that contributes to soul winning, music that reaches the masses of common people and moves their hearts, attracts the unsaved and urges them to turn to God in repentance.

There is no reason why an orchestra cannot be used to attract thousands of souls for Christ. Why can't a trombone or banjo or cornet be used in service? I thank God for Brother Trent, a renowned musician who used his trombone for the glory of God.

Don't you think the "Hallelujah Chorus" would reach more people if they would say it sometimes rather than sing it? Don't you think that the mood of the heart ought to be reflected in the music, and heart praises ought to be reflected in the face and in interpretation? And the pleading of an invitation song ought to be Spirit filled pleading. Unfortunately, our churches do not have songs that are Spirit filled; and therefore they will never be used to win any souls.

8

SUNDAY SCHOOL
IN THE BLACK CHURCH

Sad as it may sound, most pastors of black churches don't even go to Sunday school. Most pastors get to church after Sunday school is over, to perform during the 11 o'clock service hour. One pastor I know told me that Sunday school is for children. Another said that he hated Sunday school when he was a boy. He said he never got anything out of it and therefore he has never gone since he started to preach.

The average black pastor is so concerned about what he is going to say when all the folk come to church that he doesn't have time for these "little things." He is often afraid that if he says something in Sunday school it may take away from his effectiveness during the 11 o'clock service. This type of preacher has no interest in what is happening in the Sunday school.

On the other hand, do you know that in a lot of churches the superintendent is a little pastor and does not stay for church? This is especially true if he thinks he knows more or has better judgment than the pastor.

In many churches in the South the Sunday school is a virtually separate organization. The superintendent and one or two missionary women run everything. They order the literature, raise money so that they may be represented in the Sunday school and B.T.U. Congress, give scholarships to their pupils, and so forth.

In many churches the Sunday school session is not considered a "service" but the teaching aspect of the church. In reality the Sunday school is the church teaching rather than the teaching aspect. The 11 o'clock hour is the church preaching aspect of the service.

HAVE YOU EVER NOTICED

You probably have never thought of the fact that more sinners, more potential leaders, robbers and murderers, gangsters, and so forth, come to Sunday school than to any other part of the service. You probably have never noticed that you have an excellent opportunity to reach the whole family in Sunday school, whereas in the women's organization you can reach only the women or in the men's organization you can reach only the men. Now that these facts have been called to your attention, utilize your Sunday school to reach men, women, boys, and girls alike for Christ. There are many people today who are functioning for God who were saved in the Sunday school.

You can reach more people through Sunday school than you can through any other single or combined program in the church. Jesus said that we are to carry the gospel "to every creature." This can best be carried on through the Sunday school.

Here in Inkster we try very hard to organize our whole church for evangelism. Brother Charles Johnson, superintendent of the junior and junior high department, mentioned the fact that he has set several weeks for his whole Sunday school to visit. Through this kind of effort in a department the whole Sunday school can become the department of church visitation.

We feel that it is the pastor's responsibility to organize an effective Sunday school to reach souls for Jesus Christ, and that he has the same responsibility to supervise the Sunday school as he does the church.

WHAT ABOUT BLACK SUNDAY SCHOOL TEACHERS

In most black churches, the Sunday school teacher is usually a likable person with pleasant personality, or a pseudointellectual who thinks that he fits perfectly into God's work simply because he might have a little training or a little interest. Many teachers who feel that they are pretty good Bible scholars do not attend the worship hour. In many cases there is no stress on

64

real conversion by the pastor, no mention of soul winning, and no visitation program whatsoever.

To my surprise, one of the boards of deacons in a small city voted that a Sunday school teacher did not have to come to Sunday school teachers' meeting in order to be a teacher. In this church, there would be no way possible for the pastor to start a uniform promotion program or a visitation program. This church of course is only interested in maintaining a fairly good social club and not an active Spirit filled church.

It would be so wonderful if every department in a Sunday school would do all it could to win several souls during a particular month. Each department could set aside a day during a month or a quarter to have a "decision day." This is a day in which every department of the church would try to win at least ten souls for Christ and have them walk the aisle during the 11 o'clock hour. If you have three departments in your Sunday school, you ought to have thirty souls for the Lord.

The point herein expressed is that Sunday school is an excellent place to win souls for the Lord Jesus Christ. A teacher must have a burden for lost souls, she must live the life she teaches, and she must visit absentees. Not just a phone call or a postcard will do, but a personal visit from the teacher! And if the young people's or adults' class is too large to enable the teacher to look after all the visitation, then the class should be divided into sections. Each section should have a leader or chairman who will be responsible to see that every absentee in his section is visited. I know that some Sunday school teachers think a postcard or phone call is enough, but that is not the plan of the New Testament nor of the great Sunday schools in America. It takes work. It takes hard work!

If there are many absentees, it may first seem to be an impossible job. But visiting will help secure regular attendance and will gradually cut down the number of absentees. And, teacher, you must account to God for those enrolled in your class for getting them saved, getting them enlisted in the church, getting them baptized. We must teach the Word, teach them to tithe, to pray, to read the Bible, and to win souls.

LET'S CHANGE

What we need in most black churches is a change from a meaningless Sunday school to one of vigor and vitality for the Lord Jesus.

If you have a visitation program, people will criticize you and will accuse you of moving into their territory. So many times I have been accused of stealing other people's members. An old preacher said, "The world is my parish. We don't take any sheep but we will steal all the goats we can." I will make no agreement with any pastor, church, or ministerial association to limit my ministerial outreach.

If a man, woman, or child is a member of or a regular attendant at some Bible-believing, soul-winning church, well and good. Of course, the church ought not pull people away from another Biblically sound church. But if one is unsaved and is not a regular attendant at any other church, then every Christian of any church has the solemn duty to try to win that person to Christ and to enlist him in Christian service. There is a question that black preachers must ask themselves: Am I more concerned with what the brethren think about me, what another church thinks about me, or what Jesus Christ who commanded me to go thinks about me? Remember that Jesus told us to carry the gospel to "every creature."

If one is a member of a false cult or a member of a liberal church where the gospel is not preached, why should you not try to win such a person to Christ?

Movement usually creates friction. Successful soul winning creates jealousy. But stay with God and do His will, and God will certainly give you the victory.

9
THE BLACK CHURCH
CAN BE RELEVANT

The black church traditionally has been a church designed to practice and perform spiritual gymnastics, with no real emphasis on doing what the Lord has said to do—win lost souls. It is for this reason that many of our youth who have now been exposed to a larger and more complex society than home, church, and school have offered them, have dropped out of church and consider it as being irrelevant.

Too many of our churches get on the bandwagon of socialism, which means that when a particular social issue dies, the whole church dies with it. Instead, if the church would preach and teach God's Word like the Jerusalem church did in Acts 5:42, our communities would have a deeper appreciation for the church and her ministry in our society.

It is the desire of our church to develop and spread a concept of an umbrella of spiritual concern over the whole city. We are trying to develop focal points where a broader span of spiritual activities can take place as you will see in the chapter entitled "Saturation Evangelism."

We would like to make it absolutely clear that we are not suggesting that you establish miniature churches in the various parts of your city. Rather, the purpose is to design specific ministries to meet the needs of a particular area. For example, in a deprived area where many young people are failing in school, the black church can provide tutoring sessions where Christian young people (as well as adults) try to help the failing learn to study and to achieve success in school. This can be done in the name of Christ.

In a like manner, the church can establish groups in sewing, family nutrition, medical self-help (first aid), various crafts, literacy training, music, and directed recreation. Each activity can be approached as a fundamental Christian ministry and could include a brief Bible study time. This would be a weekday program.

The pastor in the black church needs more lay participation in the various facets of the church's program. Many blacks feel as if they are doing God a favor and the pastor a superfavor if they make it to church once or twice a month. In making our churches relevant our lay people must use their special training and talents in the service of God and man. They must learn to appreciate a church that will give them an opportunity to serve God through their professional or vocational training. After all, every talent belongs to God (Ps. 24:1).

The heart of the approach is that the black church will bring together all peoples of a community into the one body of Christ.

The black church through Bible giving (tithes) can go into an area where poverty abounds and sickness is prevalent, and there establish a Christian medical center. Black Christian physicians, medical students, nurses, technicians, administrators, and pharmacists can give their time and skill to examine and treat the poor. Local hospitals could continue to take all emergency needs such as surgery or critical illness, without red tape or delay coming from the Christian medical clinic. A system could be worked out where dental, orthopedic, and pediatric referrals could be cared for at the various clinics. All of this could be done in the name of Christ.

In addition to the medical clinic, there could be established a central clothing supply. Used clothing could be sorted, repaired, and fitted for those in need.

The black saved psychiatrist, psychologist, or social worker could through his church establish a Christian counseling center. Appointments could be scheduled through the church office.

The black church must extend itself beyond four walls and establish Christian day schools to develop our people physically, emotionally, socially, and spiritually. We must establish a ministry to older people who are in our communities, teaching them to lead songs and devotional services. We must be willing to listen to, encourage, and perform simple personal services for our senior citizens. Our church must provide Christian day camps to build character, as we seek to deal with the spiritual and emotional needs in the individual boy and girl. Every black church could utilize the bus ministry to bring boys and girls, men and women, to the church of Jesus Christ to hear the Word of God, taught and preached in a fundamental, Bible-believing way.

These few suggested ministries are possible only if the rich or educated black, like the poor black, dedicates himself to Jesus Christ and the purpose of the church. Black laymen must exercise Christian vision and statesmanship. We must be ready to innovate, change, and make steps forward.

Every black church layman must recognize that the church of Jesus Christ is obligated to God to attempt to reach every person in Jerusalem with the gospel of Jesus Christ (Acts 5:28).

Yes, indeed! The black church can be relevant. Your church can be a living example—our church is becoming an example. Your church, however, must be willing to suffer to break out of the mold of tradition for the cause of Jesus Christ with the winning of lost souls.

Remember, the implementation of the kind of program that our church needs cannot take place on twenty-five or fifty cents per Sunday, or with chitterling dinners, popcorn sales, and so forth, but must be carried out with tithes and offerings (Mal. 3:8-10). There must be enough money to hire a qualified, dedicated staff to represent the pastor in specific functions. Each staff member must serve under the supervision of the pastor. The pastor must be given the right to hire and fire staff members whenever he deems it absolutely necessary. Staff members should be skilled in their tasks and given creative freedom to accomplish their objectives. Each should develop his area or else should be replaced by a more competent, loyal person.

10
SATURATION EVANGELISM

"Saturation is preaching the gospel to every available person at every available time by every available means." There must be a saturated population. In order to build an aggressive church, the Word of God must be spread to the people, says Dr. Jerry Falwell of the Thomas Road Baptist Church of Lynchburg, Virginia. I heard Dr. Falwell say these words from his pulpit in Lynchburg, America's fastest growing church, according to *Christian Life*'s annual Sunday school report (September 1971).

Dr. Falwell further stated in the conference I attended in June 1971 that these days of great potential and population explosion give every church an unlimited field of souls to reach for Christ. The local church is the instrument of our Lord to bring the gospel of salvation to everyone in the world. The local church should be the launching pad for evangelistic ministry, soul winning, disciple enlistment, and Christian training.

Today there is a need for Bible centered, Christ exalting, aggressive local churches that will reach lost people for Christ.

This is exactly what we are trying to do at our local church, Second Baptist, in our local Jerusalem—Inkster. We have put together a program that we feel every black pastor ought to implement in order to reach as many lost souls as he possibly can for the Savior. We call this program "Saturation Evangelism." Our program is based on the entire Book of the Acts of the Apostles. Our preaching staff decided on the following blueprint to reach blacks of Inkster and perhaps the greater Detroit area.

EVANGELISM THROUGH THE SUNDAY SCHOOL

The right kind of organization is essential and fundamental to any thriving institution. The Sunday school must have the right kind of staff—a staff dedicated to the purpose of winning lost souls for Christ. If a member will not witness, he should be dropped from the staff of the Sunday school.

Our Sunday school teachers are our greatest soul winners. They call on visitors and absentees, and do house-to-house surveying.

Our students are encouraged constantly to invite visitors to our Sunday school. The student knows that our Sunday school is the church teaching.

Generally speaking, our Sunday school makes

contact with lost people, witnesses to them (Acts 1:8), motivates them to attend church, and brings them to hear the pastor preach the gospel of Jesus Christ. We believe that evangelism is the task of all believers—not just because it takes all of us to saturate, but because witnessing is inherent in Christian living (Matt. 5:13).

The black pastor must lead the Sunday school while helping his people develop as good teachers and good evangelists.

CORAL RIDGE EVANGELISM

Our church also uses part of the Coral Ridge program, which is called "Gospel Explosion," to build lay evangelists. Through this program we are hoping that we can eliminate sporadic forays, and develop a systematic ongoing program that will result in total coverage and long-range follow-up. (Evangelism in depth relies heavily on the systematic, door-to-door concept.)

We want to penetrate every major stratum of society. We want to go into the public mainstream with the gospel.

BUS MINISTRY

Our church presently has ten buses and eight bus routes. Through saturating our Jerusalem with buses, we have been able to bring in many boys and girls, men and women who would not otherwise attend our church due to lack of transportation.

Also as a result of this service, several hundred people have come down the aisle to Jesus in our church services. Many have been won in the home by a soul winner. Many others have been brought to church by one of the bus ministers and have been saved by the preaching of the Word.

The bus ministry increased our attendance right away, and gave our church an opportunity to invest in one of the best home mission projects possible. It provided a good place to work and to develop as effective soul winners. There are several outstanding books on the market to tell one all he needs to know to start a bus ministry: *All About the Bus Ministry*, by Wally Beebe; *Church Bus Handbook*, by Jack Hyles, and so forth.

PRINTING MINISTRY

The main purpose of the printing ministry is to provide decent Christian literature for our communities.

We started this ministry with a simple gospel tract that invited black boys and girls to come to Christ and to our church. Since that time we have put out many different kinds of tracts and promotional materials.

We now have a missionary group that carries tracts to the hospital weekly for distribution to the sick.

We have *The Informer* newspaper that we mail out each week to about two thousand homes. We are increasing the number of homes we reach daily; and it is our desire to reach five thousand homes in 1973, ten thousand in 1974, and twenty thousand in 1975, and so forth.

We mail pamphlets to every visitor to our church, and occasionally we try to blanket our entire area with a message from Second Baptist.

We also use the newspaper of our city for some advertising and Christian exposition.

TELEVISION

Our church recently signed a contract with one of the local television stations to broadcast every week. Our program, entitled "The Fundamental Gospel Time," is shown at 5:00 o'clock on Sunday afternoon.

We believe that almost every family has a television set; and since our church is the only black church in our area with a television program, we are sure to reach our Jerusalem with the gospel. It is our prayer that we can expand our television outreach by 1973 to include about ten television stations. It is also our prayer that while we are expanding we can purchase equipment of our own to tape our services from our new sanctuary.

EDUCATIONAL MINISTRY

Our old building will be used as a day care center for young children, and we intend to teach the Word of God to them while they are learning basic concepts about living. We have approximately eighteen thousand square feet in this building.

Our church is starting the Evangel Bible Temple Schools to teach the Word of God daily as an integrated part of every subject. We are starting this school by January 1973 to include kindergarten through sixth grade, adding two grades each year until we are able to provide adequate facilities for kindergarten through high school.

Along with the student getting solid Christian training, he will also get an excellent education that is superior to that of the public schools. Discipline will be maintained, therefore not allowing dropouts or expelled boys and girls much of an opportunity to attend.

We are also starting the Evangel Bible College (an evening school), which will specialize in the ministry of the local church. This vision was given to me as I traveled to several cities in America looking for a saved musician and a saved youth worker. For example, at Arkansas Baptist College, I discovered that too few blacks know the New Testament church. I found only one young man, a freshman, who was even interested in the ministries; only two at Philander Smith College, and their thinking was much too liberal for a Bible-believing church.

We intend to train black young men and young ladies for the ministry in the local church. We have talked with several outstanding Christian men about heading such a program, but we have not yet decided who will fill this position.

SENIOR CITIZENS

It is our desire to minister to people from the cradle to the grave, and therefore for the senior citizens we have the Keen-age Club.

Pastor Watson, one of my assistant pastors, has a Bible class weekly with this group, taking them on fishing trips, shopping, ball games, and so forth.

We are going to build a Senior Citizens' Housing Project for those who have nowhere to go. It will include a restaurant, barber shop, beauty shop, and other types of stores to accommodate our senior citizens.

YOUTH MINISTRY

We do not sacrifice spirituality and the Word of God for sociability. One major purpose in all programs is to get the Word of God over to our youth.

To help us reach this goal we utilize the AWANA Clubs, the young Christian Guild, for music and conferences, field trips, the Sunday school, summer recreation, vacation Bible school, camp, Bible class, visitation, and so forth.

Some of our best soul winners and bus workers are our youth. We are building a gymnasium and a swimming pool along with the new sanctuary.

We use the various methods of soul winning described above to reach the lost person for Jesus Christ. And there are still many roads to soul winning to be explored.

Let us join hands, brothers and sisters, in our community, to promote the cause of Christ with "Saturation Evangelism."

11
MIRACLES
THAT TOOK PLACE

It was in December of 1969 that I moved to Inkster as the pastor of Second Baptist Church. Since that time our ministry has been one of many miracles. We have followed the mighty hand of God in all of our endeavors.

Second Baptist had been split and was at a low ebb spiritually. Attendance was down to around sixty in Sunday school and three hundred for the preaching service. There was hardly any money and very little real equipment with which to start a church program.

The church had about three thousand dollars when I was called to pastor. Two thousand of it was used as a down payment on their first parsonage. The remainder of the money was used to move my family to Inkster and to turn on the utilities for the newly acquired parsonage. Since the church had only about six tithers and not over three or four people who would give as much as three or four dollars a week, the money came in very slowly. Our total tithes and offerings would be about three hundred dollars per Sunday.

We went to a local bank and borrowed five thousand dollars to start our new church program. We were fortunate in those days because the former pastor had led the church to pay off the mortgage on the building that we occupied.

They collected about fifteen hundred dollars at my installation program, and presented it to me. I took all of that money, invested it in our first grey and white bus and started the first real bus ministry in a black church. Other black churches had buses, but they were used to transport choirs over the country to sing. This was the beginning of our bus ministry or our bus miracle. God touched one of the outstanding pastors in our area, Pastor Downs of Gilead Baptist Church, to sell two buses to us for a total of only four hundred dollars. We bought these two, giving us a total of three buses. I then decided to take some of my own money and buy another bus.

People in our church begin to give money, until today we have ten buses. If a black pastor has a burden to reach lost souls through the bus ministry, even though the people might not understand why he will want so many buses, God will open the way.

We started the first full-time soul-winning program in a black church on January 9, 1970. We started to soul win—visiting from door to door. We were not nearly as organized as we should have been, but we were burdened for lost souls. People didn't know what to think, for *soul winning* was a brand new term. *Evangelism* was a familiar term, but soul winning was never heard of before.

As pastor I told the people that I would like to see our average Sunday school attendance of sixty-two increase substantially in 1970. We set a goal for February 22, 1970, of three hundred. We started to work very hard. Brothers Cooper and Radcliff, Sisters Harris and Pruitt, and Rev. Moss went out every day. We visited and visited. Would you believe that February 22—when Rev. Moss was hospitalized in room 591—we had 591 in Sunday school!

God continued to bless us, and we ended up with an average of about 327 for the year of 1970. We did many unusual things to promote attendance. Then came 1971, a year of test and trouble for Second. We were pondering and puzzling as to what new thing we could do. We had had a demonstration in Lansing to support the governor's drug program, a tent meeting on our worst street, Harrison, where many drunks and prostitutes and anything you look for hang out. Yet God blessed us with lost souls and many, many listeners. We reached our record Sunday school attendance with every kind of promotion that we could think of. Yet we faced our challenging '71, and drew a record Sunday school attendance of 903, on Easter Sunday 1971. We carried 600 or more in Sunday school twice during the summer season. But on December 19, 1971, God blessed us with a record Sunday school attendance of 1,226. Even though this is a tremendous record in the black church, it is nothing compared to the New Testament church where literally thousands heard the gospel.

After noticing that our membership through visitation was continuing to grow, we started to talk about adding on to our church. After an investigation by professionals, we prayed to God that He would "let His will be done." Well, God showed me eight acres of land located on the southeast corner of Michigan Avenue on Inkster Road (Michigan Avenue-Detroit goes all the way to Michigan Avenue-Chicago). I prayed over this matter, feeling that perhaps Second would not want to do that. But after much prayer the church voted to build, giving me the right to do all the negotiating for the land as well as for the building.

We paid down on eight acres of land without any money; that is, we were able to resecure the land without making a cash deposit. We then consulted an architect to do some drawings for us on our newly acquired land. We informed him that we would invest over $650,000, in Phase I of our program. We raised $350,000 in a sale of first mortgage bonds. We presented our plans to the city planning commissioners on an individual basis before going to the formal meeting. All of them thought that our plans were great and agreed right away to support this most worthwhile plan for our city. Would you believe that they then all voted against a church on this property in the formal meeting?

As a result of their votes, we were cast into a year-long struggle with the city of Inkster for a building permit in order to construct our new church on our newly acquired site. They claimed that a church could not be built in the present zoning, and that they would not under any circumstance consider rezoning the property. After a careful examination of the local zoning ordinance, I discovered that the city of Inkster arbitrarily, capriciously, and unreasonably excludes all church construction from its properties. The zoning ordinance stated that a church could be built only in a residential area (zoned multiple) with a major thoroughfare (with a 120-feet rideaway) near the property, either abutting or where access is easily available. The trick to the ordinance was that there wasn't any major thoroughfare anywhere in the city other than where our property was located, and yet we could not build there because this property was zoned for community business. The second trick to the ordinance was that a theater, an assembly hall, a movie, a school, a church, or similar structures could go in that zoning if either operated for profit. Nothing could be constructed in that zoning that had received a not-for-profit status by the state of Michigan.

Well, we decided after about six months of trying to resolve this problem on a local level to appeal to the circuit court for a decision. Our case initially revealed everything was in the city's favor. Our people became despondent and bewildered. We ended the case and the judge told us that he would hand down a decision. We waited almost six months and we finally got a decision from the judge in our favor. To me, this was the greatest miracle of the year.

God guided us through many, many miracles. Our church began to sell various items to raise money to support its programs. The Lord touched me one Sunday and asked that I would not follow the traditional pattern in church support, but that I should lead our people only in the Bible's way—tithes and offerings. Since we have followed God's way of church support, our offerings have increased more than 500 percent.

One day my assistant and I were discussing the possibility of doing our church printing, involving a newspaper and many brochures of all descriptions. We recognized that we needed a great deal of equipment and that we didn't have any money. Well, somehow we managed to get nearly two thousand dollars. We used all of this money to start our printing ministry. As a result, many people have received countless gospel messages because of this printing miracle.

There have been many, many other unusual things that have taken place at Second. For example, a body was healed of an illness, families have been united at the altar, a Sunday school student won his dad to Christ, the start of the television ministry, and many other wonderful things. To God we give all of the honor and credit!

The "meditation line" service, for which we provide a different message two to three times a week, has given much inspiration to untold numbers of people.

We have learned to lean and depend on the following Scripture verses for our miracles in the black church: "He that spared not his own Son, but delivered him up for us all, how shall he not with him also freely give us all things?" (Rom. 8:32); "But they that seek the Lord shall not want any good thing" (Ps. 34:10); "For our light affliction, which is but for a moment, worketh for us a far more exceeding and eternal weight of glory" (II Cor. 4:17); "And, behold, I am with thee, and will keep thee in all places whither thou goest, and will bring thee again into this land; for I will not leave thee, until I have done that which I have spoken to thee of" (Gen. 28:15).

12
OBSTACLES TO SOUL WINNING IN THE BLACK CHURCH

As we read the Book of Acts, one of the most impressive things we find is that the New Testament Christians were scattered abroad everywhere preaching the Word. Nearly two thousand years later, we find the most pressing problem in the black church is that of soul winning or visitation. As I travel across America I find that our churches not only fail to practice this New Testament pattern but often have never heard of this practice of the church.

The black church is known throughout her community for everything except soul winning. The churches that talk about being saved or being holy usually refer to physical perfection or keeping the Ten Commandments. The average black pastor in our communities contributes the greatest obstacles to soul winning either because he is not attuned to true Bible teaching or because he does not have a burden to see people saved. As a result, he produces people who are desensitized to the true Bible—people who have no compassion for the lost sinner.

Our services are great meeting times for fellowships, for sermons, for singing, and for praying; but they are not geared to win the lost soul. Every sermon, of course, cannot be a sermon just to win the lost; for there must be sermons of doctrine, consecration, dedication, stewardship, faithfulness, and so forth. But every service should have an evangelistic appeal, with an invitation for sinners to be saved.

In our churches the pastor will often preach a good sermon, the choir will sing a thrilling song, and people will cry, shout, and holler. Usually the choir will sing fifteen rounds of the same verse, followed by only a one-minute invitation. The pastor does not give a strong evangelistic appeal, and that creates an obstacle to building a soul-winning church. Evangelism is simply not a part of the atmosphere of most of our churches. Far too many of our people think that being a deacon or a choir member is the biggest job in the church. People should constantly be reminded that the greatest job in the New Testament church is bringing people to Jesus Christ. If we as pastors will magnify the job of soul winning above any other job in the church, then the people will get the real meaning of church and evangelism from us.

The black pastor has taught our people, perhaps subconsciously, that each person has a job to do in the church. Some are presidents, some deacons, some nurses, some ushers, some choir members, some willing workers, and so forth. This is certainly a detrimental thing, an obstacle for building a soul-winning church. Every Christian is commanded to be a soul winner; soul winning is every Christian's job. It is wrong for a person to think that operating the business of the church is his particular special field and that is all. Every Christian is to lost souls as every fireman is to a fire. Jesus said, "Follow me and I will make you fishers of men." Can you follow Jesus without fishing? Every phase of our church life must be permeated with an atmosphere of evangelism, and every leader of our church should be reminded that his main job is that of bringing sinners to Christ.

The black church must change its calendar to become a soul-winning church. When I first came to Second Church, every group raced to the pastor's office to ensure themselves of a particular night for meetings and a particular time of the year for its anniversary celebration. Our church had at least two different kinds of activities going on each evening for seven days a week. This, to them, was a proper, busy church.

But a church must be busy at its main task—soul winning. Too often auxiliaries make people so busy at lesser tasks that they have no interest, time, or energy to be active soul winners. It is like going to a restaurant that serves you so many delicacies before the meal that you are almost too full for the main course. A church that is too highly organized will not train effective soul winners. A church that keeps the people working on smaller tasks too much will have a difficult time training effective personal soul winners. A church that has too much going on uses too many week nights for other things beside soul winning and will have a difficult time training soul winners.

We must deal with another great obstacle of our church: the lack of a Spirit filled Christianity. We have plenty of emotion and plenty of religion, but not much Spirit filled Christianity in our church. For far too long, most of our Christianity has been in our mouths, in our hands, and in our feet—not in our hearts. As a result, we do not go to God and ask Him to fill us with the Holy Spirit so that we can become witnesses for Jesus Christ (Acts 1:8). If one is led by the Spirit of God he will become a new, conforming transformist as recorded in Romans 12:1, 2: "I beseech you therefore, brethren, by the mercies of God, that ye present your bodies a living sacrifice, holy, acceptable unto God, which is your reasonable service. And be not conformed to this world, but be ye transformed by the renewing of your mind, that ye may prove what is that good, and acceptable, and perfect, will of God."

It is so important that the life in our church, the main job in our church, the heartbeat of our church, the wheel of our church, and every activity of our church be built on soul winning and reaching people for Jesus Christ. Too many of our people are on a spiritual merry-go-round.

They spend all their time going around in circles and getting off right where they got on. As a result they get absolutely nowhere.

Oh, my friends! I have found that we have very few people who are really saved, dedicated, and committed to the cause of Christ. We have a great number of people who love a church building, may even love the church a little bit, enjoy the auxiliary they are members of; but very few love Jesus Christ. Until our lazy people become committed to Christ and work for Him, these great obstacles will forever stand in the way of building a soul-winning program in the black churches.

13
OUR PREACHING MUST CHANGE

Our preaching for the most part is emotional and is not evangelical. The preacher who tries to eliminate emotion altogether does so because he is not equipped with the kind of voice that the emotional preacher has. The cold sermons are usually filled with philosophy, sociology, or history, and do not reflect solid thinking or sound, fundamental, evangelical preaching.

The Holy Bible speaks to us about this matter of preaching in II Timothy 4:1-5, where it states:

> I charge thee therefore before God, and the Lord Jesus Christ, who shall judge the quick and the dead at his appearing and his kingdom; Preach the word; be instant in season, out of season; reprove, rebuke, exhort with all longsuffering and doctrine. For the time will come when they will not endure sound doctrine; but after their own lusts shall they heap to themselves teachers, having itching

ears; And they shall turn away their ears from the truth, and shall be turned unto fables. But watch thou in all things, endure afflictions, do the work of an evangelist, make full proof of thy ministry.

This message is given to pastors as Paul encourages Timothy in I Timothy 1:3. What Paul was saying in essence is that pastors are to be soul winners. The belief in most black churches is that the evangelist is the man to make the church grow, to win souls, and it is the pastor who merely feeds the sheep; but there is nothing like that taught in the Bible, nothing like that in God's program and plan. The greatest soul winners have been pastors.

Any pastor who is interested in God's program must do the work of an evangelist. If he has gifts of the Spirit they should be used primarily for winning lost souls. Some preachers will say, "Well, I am going to be just a good teacher." God intends that you teach as a pastor; but He also intends that you dedicate, consecrate, and separate yourself for the purpose of winning lost souls.

OUR PREACHING MUST ATTACK SIN

The black preacher of yesterday was a fundamental, hell-fire and brimstone preacher. He was no sissy in the pulpit. Our preachers today, on the contrary, center their messages around what the folk want to hear.

If I was asked what kind of preaching is most

94

needed in our communities, I would answer, first of all, preaching that is against sin. People will respect you and listen to you if you preach against sin.

We need to preach like Elijah. He hated sin. Listen to his prayer: "Take the prophets of Baal . . . ," and he took them down to the brook and slew them himself. Everywhere this preacher went he was known as a hard preacher. When he told Ahab that God would destroy every man of his whole family and the kingdom would be changed, Elijah was known as God's man, preaching against sin. That is the way a Bible preacher preaches.

There are other Biblical characters who preached against sin, men like Jeremiah, John the Baptist, and Peter. Not only did *they* preach against sin, but Jesus Himself denounced sin at every opportunity He got. In the twenty-third chapter of Matthew He calls the scribes and Pharisees hypocrites. Seven times He says it: "Woe unto you, scribes and Pharisees, hypocrites." He calls them "whited sepulchres." He calls them "blind." He says: "Fill ye up then the measure of your father, ye serpents, ye generation of vipers, how can ye escape the damnation of hell?"

Brother preachers, we must speak boldly against sin and point out that there is a place called hell. You cannot whitewash the issue. Without preaching against sin, no preacher will reach the proud and wicked evolutionists and atheists. Somebody must preach against sin.

Sin is the point of contact between the preacher and sinner. It is God's point of contact, too. You must do something about sin. You must repent of sin and turn your heart away from it. That is the way to be saved that Jesus preached.

We need some preachers who will get involved in controversies. God has a controversy with sin. It is sin that is populating hell. It is sin that fills every graveyard, every hospital, and every jail. It is sin that turns a marriage into a wreck, blights every home, and causes divorce. We must hate sin, so that our people will repent.

Preach on the sin and adultery shown in movies. Tell people that such movies are corrupting our youth. Most of today's movies are made by vile, evil people, holding up rotten moral standards, breaking down respect for marriage and pure love, and shunning the Word of God. Denounce the crime, the bawdy vulgarity of such movies! Preach against lodges. Tell the people that God commands Christians: "Come out from among them and be ye separate."

Preach against evolution and false cults. Preach on death, sin, hell, and judgment. Such preaching with boldness, with love, with tears, with Scripture verses, with faith, will bring great revivals and will save hardened sinners.

Some preachers preach only about the love of God. While it is good to preach about God's love, we ought to preach also about the wrath of God. The Bible says, "God is love"; but it also says, "The wages of sin is death." Be assured that your sin will find you out. God is not mocked, for "whatsoever a man soweth, that shall he also reap."

Pastors are generally afraid to preach certain kinds of sermons to certain groups of people. Well, I preach the same kind of sermons to my people that I preach to yours. Yes, I make some mad—yes, some of the people quit giving money—yes, some of the people leave the church. Maybe I will have to leave eventually, but that's the price a servant of God must be willing to pay. John the Baptist lost his head. Stephen was stoned to death. Paul was put into prison. Jesus was crucified. May God have pity on a preacher who is not willing to suffer for real convictions.

In the black community, the preacher has lost his respect. Today's black preacher is too nice and too soft-spoken. He never hurts anybody's feelings, never offends anybody, never crosses anybody, never awakens anybody, never arouses anybody, and rarely saves anybody!

OUR PREACHING MUST SHOW A COMPASSIONATE HEART

"They that sow in tears shall reap in joy" (Ps. 126:5). The tears of a broken heart are the marks of the true soul winner. If you look for joy, go with tears. You must go and bear precious seeds, but you must have a broken heart.

The broken and compassionate heart and the humble and contrite spirit please God, attract the sinner, and make the contact between these two. This contact changes the heart and saves the soul of the sinner, and brings honor to the Savior. Consider the example set by Jesus. There has never been such a compassionate winner of men as Jesus. "He saw the people as sheep having no shepherd, and had compassion on them." He wept over Jerusalem. He sought the fallen woman to forgive her and the publican to make him a preacher. His compassion would not let Him eat. He found "meat that ye know not of" in the winning of souls. His compassionate heart would not let Him sleep, for He must needs go into a mountain and pray all night or rise a great while before day to pray for the lost. His compassionate heart would not let Him die until the repenting thief on the neighboring cross was forgiven and won to Himself and heaven.

The prodigal son was a sinner. The forgiving, grieving father was like Jesus. He was the shepherd and the son was the poor lost lamb at the mercy of the cold and the beasts. As the shepherd seeks the sheep until he finds it, rescues it, and rejoices over it, so does the follower of Jesus with the sinner.

Jesus died on the cross because He loved sinners and had compassion for lost souls. That's why He allowed men to pierce His side and nail His hands and His feet to the cross.

Paul wept over sinners. "Brethren, my heart's desire and prayer to God for Israel is, that they might be saved" (Rom. 10:1). Paul was put in prison, suffered shipwreck, was beaten, and was made to bleed because he had compassion for lost sinners.

It is necessary that we become concerned about sinners and sin. It is necessary that we spend some time weeping and crying over this matter of sin. It is necessary that we become burdened about this whole matter of sin if we want to get men, women, boys, and girls saved.

OUR PREACHING MUST BE SERIOUS

If you want the Lord's power and blessing on you in saving souls, you must be serious. You must have a certain fervor of heart that involves prayer, tears, and much preparation before delivery. You must not be hung up on just how you look or how you sound or whether you preach like some seminary professor told you how to preach. You must have the Holy Spirit in your preaching. Your people must learn that their pastor is sincere and that he means business for God.

Even though to some I might appear to be overly critical about our preaching and our church (because I am straightforward and tell it like it is), I do feel that we have a great trait that's needed in order to become good evangelical preachers, and that trait is sensationalism. I try to be sensational, and I don't mind being criticized for being so. People criticized Peter and Paul and Barnabas. "These that have turned the world upside down are come hither also." Remember, Peter and John were dragged before the Sanhedrin and the priest said, "Ye have filled Jerusalem with your doctrine." When there is a riot and a preacher gets slammed into jail, when someone spits in his face and he is the target for rotten eggs and tomatoes, and still through it all drunkards, harlots, convicts, and dopeheads are saved, then you have a sensation.

Sensation is representation of the boldness of God, the fire of the Spirit, and the kind of preaching that will make men fall on their knees and repent of their sins.

WE MUST USE EVERY SERMON FOR SOUL WINNING

If you preach a funeral, give an invitation. There are many, many unsaved people who will come to a funeral. If all are saved at the funeral, then ask the saints to win a soul before the next funeral. If you conduct a wedding, speak of Christ and give an invitation. Someone usually needs to be saved in that kind of a gathering also. Wherever you go, regardless of the occasion, sneak in Christ and the plan of salvation in some way. You say, "Well, if I do that, people will be offended." Then just announce ahead of time that this is the only kind of sermon you will preach. They will know what kind of preacher you are.

OUR PREACHING MUST BE FILLED WITH THE HOLY SPIRIT

Don't depend on magnetism, personality, or

psychology, because none of these will get souls saved.

When Jesus came to be baptized and waited and prayed, the Holy Ghost came like a dove on Him, and He was anointed (Luke 3:21-22). Then He went back and said, "The Spirit of the Lord is upon me, because he hath anointed me to preach the gospel to the poor; he has sent me to heal the broken-hearted, to preach deliverance to the captives and recovering of sight to the blind, to set at liberty them that are bruised, to preach the acceptable year of the Lord" (Luke 4:1, 16-22). Jesus never worked a miracle or preached a sermon without the anointing of the Holy Spirit.

My brother, in order to preach for results, to preach for souls, to be evangelical, you must receive an anointing of the Holy Spirit. You need power from on high. Oh, I am not talking about being a jabbler of tongues, or having an ecstatic feeling, or being of sinless perfection. I do not mean this to be a self-centered "experience" so that you may go about boasting that you are holier than another; and I do not care whether you call it a baptism, a feeling, an anointing, a powering out of the Spirit, or a gift. But may God help us to see that we need His power—power to witness so that souls will be saved and churches revived; and may God become real and His presence blessed to thousands. "Ye shall receive power after that the Holy Ghost is come upon you; and ye shall be witnesses unto me both in Jerusalem and in all

Judea, and in Samaria, and unto the uttermost part of the earth" is what Jesus promised in Acts 1:8.

Evangelistic preaching, if it is to be greatly blessed of God and is to work soul-saving miracles, must boldly attack sin, must have holy earnestness and fervor, must depend on the Word of God, must aim for definite results, and must have a definite endowment of the Holy Spirit.

The test of whether the Holy Spirit is in the church is not one of emotion or commotion, but one of devotion and commitment to the purpose of soul winning.

14
IF YOU TRY, IT WILL WORK

Jesus said in the great commission, "Go ye therefore, and teach all nations, baptizing them in the name of the Father, and of the Son, and of the Holy Ghost" (Matt. 28:19). He said, as recorded in Mark 16:15, "Go ye into all the world, and preach the gospel to every creature." God intends that every Christian obey these words.

The church at Jerusalem (New Testament church) followed the command of Jesus so completely that "daily in the temple, and in every house, they ceased not to teach and preach Jesus Christ" (Acts 5:42). They were so anxious to do God's will that they went "praising God and having favor with all the people until the Lord added daily such as should be saved" (Acts 2:47). Because they had undertaken this great burden for lost souls, the Lord added three thousand new converts to the church.

THE CHURCH MUST BE BATHED IN SOUL WINNING

The church's main emphasis must be winning lost souls for Jesus Christ. We must do everything in our churches for the glory of God. We must realize that heaven does not shout over financial rallies or singing programs, but over the church's burden to win lost souls. "I say unto you, that likewise joy shall be in heaven over one sinner that repenteth, more than over ninety and nine just persons, which need no repentance" (Luke 15:7).

Our churches ought to meet with one basic question in mind: How can we preach, sing, pray, and so forth, to win the greatest number of souls today for Jesus Christ? How can we develop soul winners throughout our church? How can we give our people a burden and a compassion for lost souls? Preachers, if we are going to get a lot of souls saved for Jesus Christ, then we are going to have to redirect our church programs and pray for a revival of our saints.

It is our desire at Second Church to make every service evangelistic. We want to see lost souls coming forward each week. Our purpose in Sunday school, Awana, with the buses, with the TV program, and many other programs is to see lost souls saved.

YOUR CHURCH SHOULD BE KNOWN FOR SOUL WINNING

A church that wins souls according to the

New Testament pattern will attempt to get the gospel to "every creature" and to carry the gospel as they did in Acts 5:42. "And daily in the temple, and in every house, they ceased not to teach and preach Jesus Christ." Therefore, your church should carefully seek to make contact with every individual possible, to enter into his joys, to praise him for success and promotion, to comfort him in his sorrow. Say a word for Jesus Christ whenever a door or a heart is open, and so let the church become known over a wide area as being full of love for the poor, for people in trouble, and a friend to every person who needs help.

God has blessed our church here in Inkster to be known for our labor in the gospel. We have won much favor with many people, and yet we feel we are merely touching the surface of what can be done for Christ in our Jerusalem. We have carried 1,226 in Sunday school on a single morning, but for some odd reason 1,226 looked more like 200 to me. Well! Maybe that's because I am looking forward to the day when our record-breaking attendance will be 12,226. Maybe I'll have to wait ten years; I don't know.

Finally, not every advance will be received kindly. Not every witness will bear immediate fruit. Some seed will fall on stony ground, and the birds of Satan will take some seed away. But some will fall on good ground. The church should set out to use every means available to meet and to love and to witness to every person in the community and beyond.